# EFFEMINATE

## *Poems: Damon Mitchell*

*For a boy I know still exists*

# BONES OF THE SKULL

1. Parietal Bone

2. Temporal Bone

3. Lambdoidal Suture

4. Soft and Fragile

5. Auditory Meatus

6. Mastoid Process

7. Thumb Rest

8. Can You See

9. The Bruises

10. The Damage

11. Where I Store It

12. Frontal Bone

13. Ethmoid

14. Cracked, Broken

15. Lacrimal Bone

16. His Hand

17. I Bite

18. And I Bleed

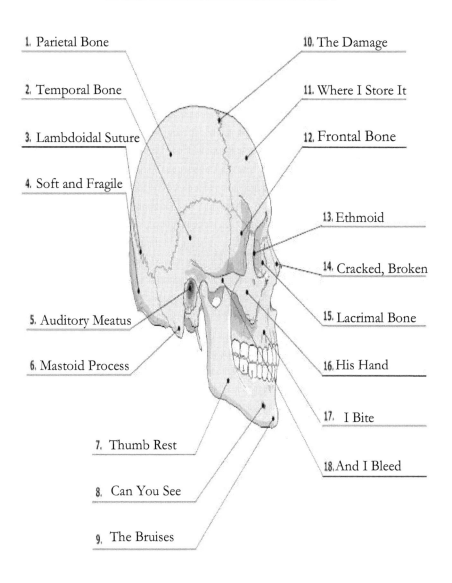

# TABLE OF CONTENTS

## OLD TESTAMENT

## NEW TESTAMENT

# OLD TESTAMENT

# Genesis

At some point God said
"Let there be light" and there was.

Somewhere. I think. Maybe,
this body just doesn't hold the sun well.

Doesn't hold God well

Maybe, somewhere, at some point
the light seeped from this skin, faded.

Lost its holy.
Gave itself over to a world

that does not believe in it.

Was this the moment it all began?
I think just maybe

# Guerilla Warfare

Everywhere I go turns itself a battlefield.
My presence is always an act of warfare.

This means,

I am always considered a public enemy,
                            a
                                        moving
                    target.

Always wondering which pair of straight hands
will attempt to rip
                    the
                    rainbows
                    from
                    my
                    mouth.
*How long will it be before they come for me?*
Emerge from sidewalk shadows with fangs bared.
Ready to tear me apart.

But more so,

how ready will they be,
*when I bite back?*

# Hennessey's Tavern

I am at a reunion
            for a school I did not attend
at some bar
            that I have never been to
in a city
            I have only seen in pictures.
The boy who invited me
is already one too many in when I arrive.

He parades me in front of his friends.

They are not amused.

Their halfcocked smiles reaffirm that
                        I am        out of
                    very        place.
I try to ignore that feeling.

Drag the boy over to the bar
and have him buy me a drink

after a few I no longer care.

I lock eyes with a hetero across the floor.
who looks at me for entertainment.

Without looking away
I pull the boy to my mouth.

If it's a show they want
so be it.

# Microaggressions

*"But don't worry, he's a cool gay"*

The words pour from her mouth. A leaking faucet that seeks to fill the empty basin between our bodies. We all laugh, Helium and Nitrous-Oxide our lungs so this shit seems less awkward, it doesn't. The rest of this conversation becomes a broken air conditioner, becomes leather car seats, becomes panting dog, straight man sweating so profusely there is a swimming pool beneath us. It's disgusting. I laugh anyway, hoping my voice can resurrect the air conditioner. Break open the car window. Provide panting dog with water long enough so he can stop staring at me like I am making him uncomfortable. It does not happen. This conversation then becomes census bureau questionnaire. Becomes comedy club humor. A pseudo-silent statue standing in proclamation of this man's fragile heterosexuality. Suddenly, I become smoke detector, become car alarm, or barking dog. I become my father's laughter as his masculinity keels over in his stomach. He tells my seven-year-old body standing in the mirror that I look too much like my mother, and not enough like a man. I laugh for the first time hoping that it will shatter glass, break the door hinge, and crush the foundation of this house. It doesn't happen. So I trade my heels in for new sneakers that in five years would plant themselves weed in the concrete of a courtyard where I do not belong. The claws of children tear at my mother's blouse adorned as a cloak on a body that I do not know how to be boy in yet. I laugh with them hoping my voice will tetherball their tongues and bury them under the blacktop. It does not happen. It was always the boys, and I learned to live with it for a while at least. At fourteen I am sitting on my mother's couch. Her body is just bones of a woman I once knew. She finds her tongue long enough to tell me that I am dead to her. Tells me that I am flickering candle flame, and she is worried if left unattended my love will burn down her house. I laugh hoping the mortar in my stomach burns down the house and wastes everything. It doesn't. So, I trade my bed for a stranger's sheets. Trying to find home in another body. Then at seventeen a man tells me that I am the cheapest blanket he has every wrapped himself in. For months he pulls loose thread form my tongue to sew my mouth shut. Tells me he prefers it if I don't laugh. It put cyanide cherry pit in his stomach. He'd rather just look at me standing in the mirror. Tells me that my body is not fit well for clothes, too big for my skin, but small enough for his suitcase. I swallow my laughter and zip tie my tongue. Think maybe my silence will save me this time. It doesn't After this, all my conversations become highway traffic, become late night tv static, become amber alerts. Things people chose to not listen to after some time. Yet, here I am so many years later. Stuck in this conversation that sounds too much like highway traffic. My tongue slams on the brakes. This man sounds too much like tv static, too much zip tied tongues and ripped sheets. He speaks and he becomes my mother's bones. He becomes children buried beneath the blacktop. He becomes my father as he breaks the door hinge, crushes the foundation of this home, and shatters a seven-year-old's heart.

Still, they wonder why I've stopped laughing this time.

# The Book of Matthew

gay boy/ with all your gap tooth glitter/ and rainbow presence/ why do you cry/ cathedrals/ to be buried in/ is this body/ not holy/ enough/ for you/ the messiah/ the prophet/ of punk rock/ and guyliner/ you the deliverer/ from the heteronormative/ you/ boy/ so small and broken/ does it hurt/ trying to hold/ all this hallowed ground/ together/ you/ graveyard/ you/ unwavering/ boy/ do you hear them/ hissing/ with forked tongue/ but are you not a snake tamer/ boy/ do you fear them/ the ways they seek you/ seek to bind you/ nail to the cross/ boy/ do you fear them/ boy/ do you fear crucifixion/ boy/ do you fear death/ boy/ do you fear yourself/ boy/ how many times/ have you tried/ ripping/ the divine/ from your wrists/ only to/ keep living/ how many times/ have you died/ before/ boy/ is this not/ the part of the story/ where you are/ brought back/ again/ resurrected/ again/ is this not where/ the earth splits open/ releases you/ sanctified/ you/ boy/ a church/ again/ unwavering/ with all of you glitter/ and gospel/ returned/ and they will come for you/ again/ and again/ and again/ do not fear them/ boy/ do not fear the cross/ boy/ do not fear death/ boy/ for/ you/ are/ the/ rapture.

# Cherries

Tongue tied cherry stems
caught between stained teeth.

*This is how we show love.*

Contorting our bodies in ways
that strain the back and the heart.

*This is what we call intimacy*

## The Plain of Shinar

My mouth is Tower of Babel.
Knows lust in every language.

This tongue is serpentine.
Slithers its way through waistbands.

I bring men to their knees in prayer
without ever needing to speak.

# The Fall of Man

He holds an apple between smirking lips.
Beckons me to sink my teeth in its flesh.
The core, I continuously convince myself,
will always be the hardest part to swallow.

Every time forgetting how the seeds
lodge themselves within my throat,
expand his branches within my body,
and then remind me that I asked for it.

Justification lies within the apple,
*doesn't it?*
Knew the outcome when I bit into it,
*didn't I?*

*"Then why are you still choking?"*

*"This is what you wanted.*

*"Isn't it?"*

# Witch Hunt

One by one count the men
They all so saltlick and sulfur.

When they see me, they see kindling.

See: Body to burn

1. A Boy.

All long legged and slicked hair
comes to visit for a while,

he does.

He was so full of dance.
Knew too well
how to make a body:
fold, or bend, or twist.

How scared I was.
How I did not move.
How I said nothing.

2. Yet Another Boy
(Not the last).

Still too young
knows
how slowly the fabric can fray

Unravel itself
and engulf those sleeping

How scared I must've been.

If only I could remember.

## 3. Not A Boy, A Man

Sometime before all the others to come

Taught me:
How to turn myself into a burial site.

I learned:
How to steal the heat from something

Store it in the back of my throat
And never let it go

He seemed so soft.

All poppy seed and sunflower
How wrong I was.

How I wasn't scared
(Why are you smiling boy)

How I danced around him.
(Stand still boy)

How I tried to my untangle throat.
(Be quiet boy)

How I still remember.
(You will not forget me boy)
(You will not forget this boy)
(You will not forget)
(Right?)

# Ain't It Just Like A Man?

A man whose profile picture is a half-naked gym selfie flexing so hard his abs are a painting of desperation incarnate sends me three pictures of his four inch penis and then asks if I'm "masc 4 masc" which is to say "I don't want you if you're feminine... please excuse the last three photos I just sent " and my femininity gags on her glass of white wine. How sad it must be to live in this loathing. You could not consume the whole of me if you wanted to. This body too grandeur, too monument for you to break down, and the next day, as I do, I have him wrapped around my tongue. His moans in my ear a begging dog. Suck the afternoon out of him, and go before he can cum. Tell him, ain't it just like a man, to leave before something is finished. He like so many others never wanted me to be masculine to begin with.

A man stands alone in the corner of a club, he a dagger wrapped in a flannel, ripped jeans, and Doc Martens. He grins, and I can already see my flesh stuck between his teeth. A cracked mirror, a ghost's reflection. Beckons me, as they do, a cat call. Tells me that for a boy I sure do have the ass of a woman and grabs a handful before I can walk. I bloody his face a slaughterhouse, stain my knuckles tombstone, the crowd watches as a pornography unravels itself on the dancefloor. Ain't this the fuck you wanted? Aggressive, and tongue-lashing. Ain't it just like a man, to beat meat, to not care?

A man, sits stranger, on a hotel bed. His dead eyes satellite in the way they search to drain the life left in the night of this room. "Be a good girl and suck a nice one for daddy." I shotgun my mouth and blow this man across the wall. His moans, his pleas, echo across the room cannon fire, this a ritual we call warfare. Me sleeping with the enemy because I, been taught this body only belongs to me if it does not belong to someone else. Been taught that something is only mine if I use it before someone else does, and ain't that just like a man? To conquer those least expecting? Ain't this masculine enough for you now? Ain't it?

# Autopsy

An autopsy is a highly specialized surgical procedure.
It is a thorough examination of a corpse, by dissection,
to determine the cause and manner of death.

When my flesh lay flayed open for the final time
I wonder, what pieces of you they will find inside me.

Still occupying space that has never belonged to you.
Tongue lodged somewhere between sternum and pelvis.
Fist turned third stage of death, caught in esophagus.
Fingerprints seared onto the rings of the trachea.

Autopsies are performed in the cases of sudden fatality.
A principal aim of which is to determine the state of health
of said corpse before he or she succumbed to death.

When the cavities of my body are dismembered again
I wonder, if the coroner will talk of my smile.

How my lips turned lapidescent long before my body.
Spirit plucked from these lungs still breathing.
Skin peeled from the waist down in sacrilegious practice
of fingers that laid to bed between thighs.

An autopsy is the work of a pathologist's blood magic.
It is the folklore of a thousand coroners who tell stories
of broken bodies that have been riddled with holes
the likes of which no one else has bared witness.

Which is to say,
no one cares when the bodies of boys are ripped open
as long as it looks surgical, if the incisions are sewn shut,
if given back to their mothers in a single piece.

Embalming is the process of preserving the corpse.
It is the prison bars that hold the decay captive
Long enough to steam and wax the carcass,
polish boy enough to present him to the public again.

I have been doing this to myself for years

Taking my tongue, and stitching it into place
Understanding how to balance the acts of
playing dead but being alive enough to look at.

Now, autopsies are nothing more than questions
lying cadaver in the casket of my mouth.
like, who gave you permission to be in my body?
Consent forms absent of my signature.

Which is to say

Autopsies are nothing more than statements,
proclaiming the purpose and state of the body
without asking the owner for permission to enter

An autopsy is a highly specialized surgical procedure.
It is the last line of the practitioner's defensive.
Ensure that the post mortem vessel is vacant of life

But

You are no pathologist.

And

I'm still breathing.

# The Morning After

And I crawl from his body, tongue too dry.
Beads of sweat roll cold against morning air
still crisp.

The sky bleeding a falsetto red
as if to say
*look child, I too know of wounds.*

And he is sleeping.
Head laid soft on a pillow, mouth agape.

Mouth so full of teeth.

Mouth an obituary waiting to be written
with the same saliva that covers my skin.

My skin,
trying to flower itself into some distant morning

Somewhere far away from the cracked leather
and stale coffee grounds.

Where the asphalt isn't as hot.
Isn't as dangerous a route

from the boys who offer me a smile
as collateral for the night and it's joyousness.

Each tooth a promise.

A reminder that this body belongs to the one with
the wettest tongue, and deepest bite.

Until it doesn't.
Until I pull my flesh from his mouth,
still dripping.

The salt rolling from my fingers
as I steal the sun and pull it into that distant morning.

One where the concrete is still cold on my feet.
Where the concrete already knows the way home.

Blessed be that concrete.
How it never leads me back to his bed.

How sturdy it must be to uphold the weight
of a morning so heavy with salvation.

*And what a morning that would be, wouldn't it?*

Wonders the mind slightly in the 6am haze.
Pulling the sheets over a body still covered in salt.

Tongue still too dry in a thirsty mouth that watches
the boy as he stays sleeping. Head laid soft on a pillow,

mouth still agape.

# A Recollection of The First Time.

My father and I are driving down the 405.
The silence burning in the glare of the 7am sun

He came to find me
                half-naked
                            skin against the pavement.

He does not ask what happened,
knows too well I will not hand over the truth.

Besides,

The silence has now unfolded itself
into its own form of this story,

One where we do not speak about:
the blood                    or
the discolored flesh         or
Wesley, the man              or
anything at all.

We just drive.
The freeway carrying us in its drift.

Two dead men
                choking on their tongues,
and I swallow so hard
                my throat collapses on itself.

Palm pressed against the pane of the window.
Stretching my fingers so wide just to feel:
the vibration            or
the heat                 or
a heartbeat              or
anything other than my body

The residue from that man's hands
still far too fresh on my skin

I wonder if my father can see the stains
how they paint me into some missing child

a boy, barely recognizable.

Just some stranger sobbing under my breath
in the passenger seat of his Chevy Cruze

The engine of which
holds me captive.

Slowly reminding me of:

a cracking bed frame

my teeth as I grind them to dust

a soft utterance of the word "no"
like a plea evaporated into nothing.

I wonder if my father can hear the screams.
The ones pressed against the roof of my mouth

If he does,
he does not mention it.

Instead, focuses on the road in front of us.

The curvature of the asphalt leading us
further into the silence
and for twenty miles

we say nothing.

Allow the heat to boil
the tips of our tongues

until there is nothing to say

anyway.

When the car finally brakes to a halt
the fresh air bites into my chest

I gasp for a moment of understanding

My father does the same.

My father a brick house
trying to keep the stone standing

as I extend "I'm sorry" out fragile in my hands.

He grabs me as if I am sand.
Tries so hard to not let me slip through his fingers

"No son" he says.

"You are alive."

## Fight or Flight

*"Did you try fighting back?"*

Despite all of this, I have still yet to learn how to explain the innate reaction to turn off all of the lights as to conserve energy. How heavy the body becomes in such a dark place. Each brittle bone just a hair weight away from reducing itself to soot. Me, shredding all of my muscle and willpower just trying to keep from disintegrating. Sometimes you just can't anymore. When fight or flight is no longer an option. When you are as small as he made me there comes a point where you release your fist, stifle your crying, and you bite the bullet, or the pillow, or your hand. At this point, you do only what you must to survive. Even if that means lying still and staying quiet. Somewhere in the recesses of my mind, I knew that one day I would shed all of this skin and stand in a body untouched. To do that though, I had to make it through the night.

*"Of course," I say, "I did everything I could."*

# Netflix and Chill?

Here I am again/ thumbing through the sadness/ like an
unanswered prayer/ that has been sent back to me/ the recipient
has changed their address/ now with nowhere to go/ it comes
home/ beds itself back into my bones/ a lonely that craves the
harshest of touch/ wants so badly to be held/ it does not consider
the cost/ like/ a lover that deems me nothing more than a fuck/
hands on my hips/ we sway in the glow of television light/ he
whispers/ presses it against my neck/ tells me that I will always be
too much/ or not enough/ and in the same breathe/ asks me to
say I love him/                I do                / my tongue always
gives in too easy like that/ so willing to hand itself over to a man/
if it means that I can keep him/ even if only for the night/ I pull
him closer/ ask the bed to debone us both/ it responds only with a
soft creaking/ says/ do what you want/ says/ use him if you must/
so I bite deeper into the boy/ ask his flesh for forgiveness/ it
responds only with his sweat on my lips/ we kiss/ and then there is
nothing/ but him and me/ and the television/ buzzing in the
background

# NEW TESTAMENT

# Hickory and Bourbon

Straight Boy laughs when I ask him
if he can walk me to my car.
He does,
but he does not understand my fear
of the dark,
of long distances,
of walking alone.

He stands at about 6'2.
Weighs nearly two hundred pounds.
Smells oddly of hickory and bourbon.
Asks me if his presence
makes me feel safer
I tell him to "fuck off."

*It does.*

That night, we stay awake too long
drinking cheap beer, and cheaper wine.
Spill secrets across the coffee table.
Discuss past lovers, and heartbreak.

Straight Boy awakens early the next day.
Stretches his limbs, and texts me at six,
just to ask me if I've made it home safely.
I tell him to "fuck off."

*I have.*

Straight Boy's name is _____,
He reminds me slightly too much of _____
the one who would shelter me from home.
Lulled me to bed so I didn't feel alone in the night

Understood I was afraid of the dark.
But did not understand why.
Still, would cascade me in candle light
Assure that I would feel warmer.

*I didn't.*

Straight Boy finds a saviour complex.
I try to find reason to blame him
Tell him I do not need saving.
Not from men in back alleys
or monsters in closets
or myself

"I know you don't"
The words pour from his hand
into my glass of wine.
He sips... slowly
with a look of bitter
as if he finally understands.

*He doesn't.*

# Halloween

There is nothing scarier in this world

than a boy who is too quick to smile at you.

Look at how all his teeth fall perfectly in line.

each one just another gravestone in the way

of his tongue, a sweet, soft spoken killer.

He will try his hardest to swallow you whole.

Try to bury you within him and then

pick out the leftovers and discard you.


Sometimes I regret being as sweet as I am.

Having become something so worth of the taking,

and now all I do is attempt to mask the sadness.

Pretend they have not torn all my softness from me.

So tonight, when he smiles, I will smile back

and act like I do not hear the gnashing of teeth.

# TIDE ™

I wash old bed sheets, in the same way
I rewrite the stories of men who have stained them.
Hoping that by removing the filth from the fabric
they too may cease to exist

# Transmogrification

Tonight, I woke up in the shape of a new body,
shed you from my skin, and rebirthed myself
into a world absent of your memory.

Broke open the birdcage of my chest,
resuscitated these lungs that have been filled
with clipped wings and broken talons.

*I could not save the Starling.*

Tonight, I learned the hardest part of recovery is
piecing the shards of mirror back together,
and finding something recognizable.

Like the alchemist reshapes matter.
Manifests it into a rejuvenated frame
without changing the contents of its core.

*I do not call this magic.*

Tonight, I smelted steel to craft new armor.
I wove a garland of Provence rose,
and adorned my flesh with pristine wings.

I have been held captive in my own body.
Caged by memories of nights of the past, and
men that have controlled me.

*No longer.*


Tonight, I am free.

# On Love and Healing

Child then asks me if I know of love.
          I tell him yes
Child asks me if love was good to me.
          I do not want to not answer.

          So I tell him of the sunflowers.
          The ones that sat in the kitchen.

          How every day I poured love into them
          and I never asked for it in return.

          Tell him that love does not
          need to be reciprocated to be good.

          It doesn't matter if it's good to you,
          as long as you are good to it in the end.

          It is then that love will come back for you.

          When the rest of the world turned its cheek
          and allowed the sadness to take me again.

          They stood bright, blooming and full of the sun.
Child asks where they went
          I tell him that eventually
          even the most loved of flowers wilts,

          and with it so too does the love go.

Child asks if I saved any for myself.
Are you not still here?
Should you not be good to yourself for once?
Are you not still blooming?

# The Magician

Love is a magician.
His favorite act: disappearing.

I am never sure if I am the audience
or the source of the magic.

But, if I am the latter,
does this mean I will disappear too?

## A Place to Rest

I lie in a lover's arms soft like the Saturday sunrise.

The light barely making itself visible through the blinds.

*Can we he hold this moment, just a little longer?*

He stretches, the world shifts as he pulls me in

His lips lie on my head as he slips slowly back to sleep.

I do realize, that eventually, I will give him back to the day.

The sun will settle and wash this away with the morning.

For now, though, I nest into his shoulder and smile.

In this moment the morning fades and nothing else matters.

# Oceans Away

There is a boy in Japan.

Okinawa or Kyoto, I forget which.

I do remember though, the day that
the world began spinning in reverse.

The ocean breaking the hold of the tide
and flooding into the room.

My hands caught too wet in the moment.

The water cascading from his mouth
as he spoke.

The ring
burning a hole into the side table.

Then everything turned ash or steam.
I forget which.

I do remember though

there is a boy,
somewhere across the ocean,

who smiles at his husband in a way
that seems all too familiar.

They kiss,
and he wipes the salt from his mouth.

I bet it tastes too much like me.

# Phosphorus

*And the match?*

What of the match?

He who is so willing
to burn his body
and relight the candle.

Breathe life back into a dead lover.
Proclaim it resurrection, name it "love."

Ignore the scars and the singed flesh.
Ignore the burn and the destruction.
Ignore all the ways that he will

*never be the same.*

# Where Can I Buy Your Love?

*After Donte Collins*

and how late do you stay open/ does it come in my size/ not one
size fits all/ I need something/ bigger/ is it on sale/ where is it/
can you check the back/ how much does it cost/ and what's the
tax/ how long will you have it/ where is it again/ I'm sorry/ could
you show me/ how long will it last/ does it stain/ how do I
remove it/ can it get dirty/ how do I clean it/ will it fade/ is there
a warranty/ is it high maintenance/ require attention/ how do you
take care of it/ I'm sorry/ could you show me/ is it organic/ all
natural/ what is it made out of/ cotton/ silk/ polyester/ is it
hypoallergenic/ is it safe to touch/ can I touch it/ what are its side
effects/ is it dangerous/ can it harm me/ will it make me sick/
what do I do then/ is there a way to prevent that/ okay good/
where is it/ I'll check back in tomorrow/ can I find it somewhere
else/ where is it/ when will you have it again/ will the price
change/ what is your return policy/ what if I don't have the
receipt/ can I have my money back/ where is it/ I can't find it/
where is it/ could you show me/ where is it/ where is it/ where is
it/ are you out?

## Grave Dressing

This soft breath, a faded whisper.
A boy I knew once cradles me in this skin.

How distant it feels to be this way.
How distant it is to be ghost.

To be apparition, laid in a bed
Waiting ever patiently for the end.

This walking corpse searching
for any remaining heartbeat,

a sign that some part of you
might still be waiting for me.

Somewhere beneath the soil
bones turn themselves mausoleum.

In the distance a gunshot rings.
Echoes and ricochets off brick walls.

I wonder what death could be occurring
as I choke on the smoke between us.

A smothered bonfire lost in a body
Sends me to bury myself in sheets.

Tell them bones to stop shaking
It ain't always this cold

and it's only going to get colder
It is

# When Repentance Fails

At some other point in time/ in some other life/ this may have
been the part/ where I asked for forgiveness/ again/ at some other
point/ I may have crawled from this skin/ unworthy/ lay this body
upon the altar/ call it an offering/ sacrifice it in the carnage/
again/ at some other point/ I would have wept on to the stone/ in
a contrite manner/ a form of penitence/ that never truly belonged
to me/ but/ this is not that time/ I do not/ live in that life/
anymore/ I am no longer/ that boy/ and this is not/ that apology/
I will not swallow my sadness/ or keep it from flooding/ around
you/ I will not repent/ for the ways/ that I cope with the grief/
how/ I continually bring myself back/ even with icy touch/ at
some other point/ I would've buried all of this/ in shallow soil/ if
it meant/ you would stay/ ask me now/ if I care

## Salvation

If I told you that my palms hold love like puncture wounds

Would you ask how long my hands have been empty?

Most don't.

Men will look and gawk, then cringe, then add another nail.

Lately, love has been iron melting in my mouth.
I have become so accustomed to my own blood
that everything else tastes like a disappointment.

I thought therefore he so loved me, and I allowed
this body to become yet another cross to bear.

All my relationships have ended like a crucifixion.
My pain on display like a sacrament.

Each time thinking it would be the last.
But ain't I been resurrected?

Ain't this love but the sweetest of sacrifice?

Ain't I still a hymnal?
Even with all the blood running from my palms

Am I not yet worthy of an eternity?

No, I think maybe not.

But I'll be damned if I save another man

before I save myself.

# Reclamation [Verb]

Acknowledging that some part of you
has been stolen and, after all this time,

taking that shit back.

# Revelations

Chemical shifts leave body in ruin.
Muscle submits itself servant to Brain.
Brain who can't call skin to breathe.
Nooses of flesh snaked around throat.
Tongue asphyxiated silent in mouth that refuses to speak.

Hieroglyph carved in bone.
Messages of salvation eyes can't read.
Open chest and call it holy.
Build alter from ribcage,
and offer heart as sacrifice to God.

Find sanctuary with brimstone fingers.
Crucifying tar palms to the edges of sheets.
Profess yourself holy. Your body biblical.
His touch, sin.
Your body a temple of martyrdom.

Sacrificing sanctity to the hands of a false idol
Pull him down from the heavens, smother him with your fist
and claim that he died in your stomach.
Drowned in acid, only to be regurgitated from your core
dipped in gold and mantled.
Reminders to this body that it is still not its own.

Use hands to spill blood and call it
Revelation.
Use hands to form brick from bone and call it
Reparations
Your body is temple meant to be built and built
again, if only to be destroyed by men

Consider me holy.

# From the Author

If you have made it this far, I would first like to say thank you. This story has been many years in the making, and it brings me great joy to finally be able to share it with you. However, please understand this story is not just my own. There are so many queer folk who share this narrative with me. While I may have grown and found some relief from many of the traumas of my life; there are people out there currently experiencing similar things to those that I have described throughout this story. If that is you, please know that you are not alone. While we may or may not know each, know that I see you. Whatever damage or trauma you are currently experiencing is not permanent. You can overcome all of this pain and anguish. Understand though, not every day will be a good one, not every battle will be won, and that is okay. It is okay to feel weak, tired, defeated, etc. It is okay, if you are not okay right now. What matters is that you don't give up, at least not forever. Whoever you are, where ever you are, you are loved. I love you.

# Resources

You are not alone. There are people here to help.

## National Suicide Prevention Lifeline:
**Phone:** 1-800-273-8255

## The Trevor Project:
**Phone:** 1-866-488-7386
**Website:** www.thetrevorproject.org

## National Sexual Assault Hotline:
**Phone:** 1-800-656-4873

## National Domestic Violence Hotline:
**Phone:** 1-800-799-7233
**Website:** www.thehotline.org

## Crisis Text-line:
**Text:** START to 741-741

## Planned Parenthood:
**Website:** www.plannedparenthood.org

26954821R00037

Made in the USA
San Bernardino, CA
23 February 2019